# ENDANGERED ENERGY

## INVESTIGATING THE SCARCITY OF FOSSIL FUELS

by Rani Iyer

Content Consultant:
David Taylor, PhD
Lecturer
Department of Physics and Astronomy
Northwestern University
Evanston, Illinois

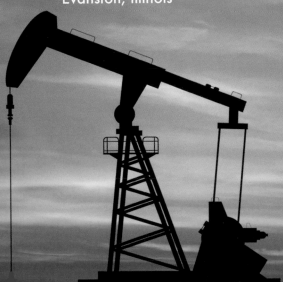

CAPSTONE PRESS

Fact Finders Books are published by Capstone Press,
1710 Roe Crest Drive, North Mankato, Minnesota 56003
www.capstonepub.com

## Library of Congress Cataloging-in-Publication Data
Cataloging-in-Publication Data is on file with the Library of Congress.

ISBN: 978-1-4914-2037-9 (library binding)
ISBN: 978-1-4914-2212-0 (paperback)
ISBN: 978-1-4914-2227-4 (eBook PDF)

## Editorial Credits

Abby Colich, editor; Bobbie Nuytten, designer; Gina Kammer, media researcher; Tori Abraham, production specialist

## Photo Credits

Corbis: © Sung-Il Kim, 8; Getty Images: John Kaprielian, 23, Katie Orlinsky, 15; Nature Picture Library: 2020VISION/Mark Hamblin, 6; Newscom: MCT/Jeff Willhelm, 16, MCT/Jon T. Fritz, 17; Science Source: Spencer Sutton, 7; Shutterstock: 1000 Words (bottom left), cover, 501room, 20, Adam J, 12, Andriano (top left), cover, artiomp, 21, Arun Roisri (bottom right), cover, Boris Sosnovyy, 28, Budimir Jevtic, 10, Condor 36, 18, Filip Fuxa, 25, Hung Chung Chih, 22, iofoto (top), 29, joyfull, 4, Matej Kastelic, 26, Nejc Vesel (bottom), 29, Paolo Bona, 19, Patrick Foto, 9, Pavel L Photo and Video, 5, pedrosala, 24, Przemek Tokar, 14, Robert Neumann, 11, Roberto Castillo, 13, thaiview (back), cover, 1, tristan tan, (top right), cover, Uwe Landgraf, 27

Printed in Canada.
092014   008478FRS15

# Table of Contents

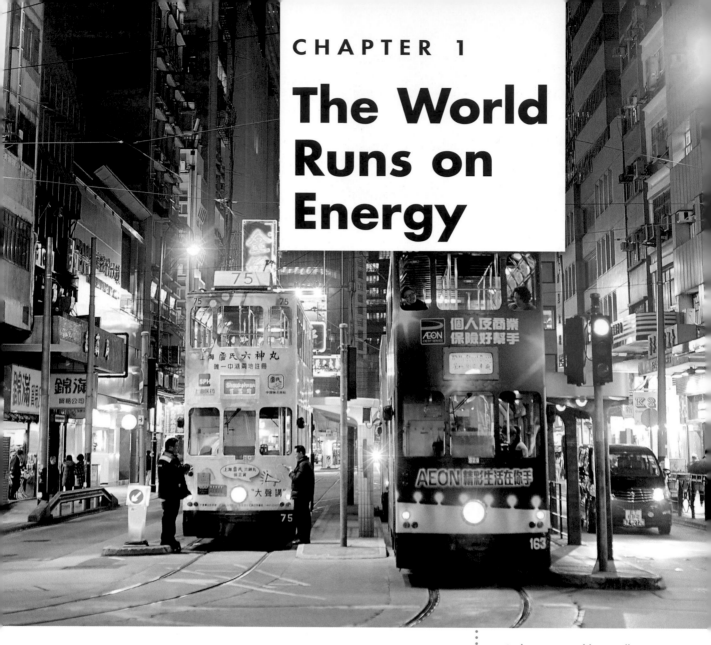

# CHAPTER 1
# The World Runs on Energy

Lights, cars, and buses all require energy to run.

Cars and buses run on **energy**. Energy keeps homes, businesses, and schools warm in the winter and cool in the summer. Energy is used to create and transport goods such as food and clothing. Energy is used everywhere. Imagine a world without it.

4

When energy is stored in objects, it is called fuel. When the fuel is burned, it gives energy. Oil, coal, and natural gas are all **fossil fuels**. Fossil fuels are the most widely used sources of energy in the world. In the United States, more than 90 percent of the energy used comes from fossil fuels. But fossil fuels will one day run out.

Electronics, including video games, use fossil fuels for power.

The oil and gas in vehicles allow travel from one place to another. Homes and schools may use natural gas for heating and cooking. The electricity that powers TV and video games often comes from coal. The uses for fossil fuels are endless. People have come to depend on these uses for fossil fuels.

People have used so much fossil fuels that they are in danger of running out. Within the next one or two centuries, some scientists believe that fossil fuels could be gone. People will be forced to find new sources of energy. And the use of fossil fuels has damaged the environment. Air is polluted. Temperatures are rising. All living beings are at risk.

**energy**—the ability to do work, such as moving things or giving heat or light

**fossil fuel**—natural fuel formed from the remains of plants and animals; coal, oil, and natural gas are fossil fuels

# CHAPTER 2

# Meet the Fossil Fuels

..... Heat and pressure inside of the Earth helped transform decaying plants and animals into fossil fuels.

Coal, natural gas, and oil were formed deep inside Earth millions of years ago. They are called fossil fuels because they were formed from the remains of plants and animals that lived long ago.

## Forming Fossil Fuels

About 300 million years ago, Earth was mostly covered with swamps. When plants and animals died, their remains sank to the bottom of the swamps. Over time mud, sand, and rock piled on top of the remains. After millions of years, heat and pressure inside Earth caused the remains to change into oil, natural gas, or coal.

The energy stored in fossil fuels originally came from the sun. Plants capture the sun's energy during **photosynthesis**. Animals eat plants and other animals. Some of this energy remained in the plants and animals when they died and were buried. When fossil fuels are burned today, that energy is released.

**photosynthesis**—the process by which plants make food using sunlight, carbon dioxide, and water

## How Fossil Fuels Form

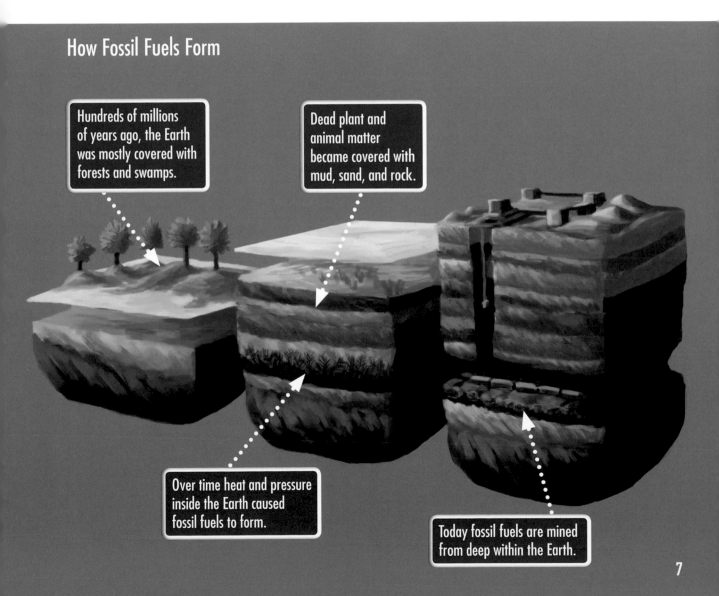

Hundreds of millions of years ago, the Earth was mostly covered with forests and swamps.

Dead plant and animal matter became covered with mud, sand, and rock.

Over time heat and pressure inside the Earth caused fossil fuels to form.

Today fossil fuels are mined from deep within the Earth.

7

## Crude Oil

Oil has been used since ancient times. More than 4,000 years ago, a type of oil was used to build the walls of the ancient city Babylon. Other ancient peoples used oil for medicine and lighting lamps.

Oil is found deep in the earth as "crude oil"—a thick yellow and black liquid. Crude oil is **extracted** from rocks below land and seas all over the world. Oil drillers must first find where oil is buried. Then a hole is drilled into the ground. A pipe is placed through the hole to suck up the oil like a straw. Oil is then taken to a **refinery**.

At the refinery crude oil is made into different products. Most crude oil is turned into gasoline for cars. Jet fuel and **diesel** fuel are also created. So are plastics and other products.

Crude oil comes out of the ground as a thick, yellow and black liquid.

# Hidden Fossil Fuels

*Thousands of items people use daily are made with oil products. Plastic bags, paint, and water bottles are all made using oil. Some crayons and clothing are made using oil. Even some chewing gum and toothpastes are products of oil.*

Oil is an important resource. Each day, the world uses about 89 million barrels of oil. That's 3.7 billion gallons (14 billion liters). Some reports state that in 50 years, oil supplies will drop greatly due to overuse. The world must work quickly to develop new ways to fuel vehicles.

**extract** — to remove

**refinery** — a place where oil is made into gasoline and other products

**diesel** — a heavy fuel that burns to make power; many semitrucks run on diesel fuel

......... At this plant workers turn crude oil into gasoline and other products.

# Natural Gas

Natural gas was discovered around 1000 BC in Greece. It was first used for heating in China around 500 BC. Today natural gas is collected through pipes and distributed to homes for heating, cooking, and to generate electricity.

Natural gas is usually found deep under layers of rock near oil. Here the Earth's temperature and pressure are very high. Natural gas is made of **methane** and other gases. It is found underground mixed with other substances. A hole is drilled deep into the rock below, and the gas is removed. Once extracted, the gas is moved in special trucks to a processing plant. Natural gas is **purified** and then transported to homes and businesses for use.

Natural gas is carefully moved through pipes and stored in tanks.

Natural gas is an important resource. In the United States, natural gas is used to heat about half of all homes. It is also used to heat water and to cook food on stoves. Many businesses and industries also rely on natural gas. The U.S. government says that natural gas will run out in about 90 years. That may seem like a long time. But it is also taking a long time to develop other energy sources.

**methane**—colorless, flammable gas produced by decay of plant and animal matter

**purify**—to make something clean

Many stoves are heated by natural gas flames.

11

## Coal

:.. Coal is a type of rock.

Coal is a black or brown shiny rock that is mined from underground. Coal was first used in China about 3,000 years ago. Ancient Romans also used coal as a source of energy. They dug for coal in England and Wales beginning around AD 200.

Today there are more than 20,000 coal **mines** around the world. Coal near the surface of the Earth is removed using digging equipment. Deeper coal is mined up to 1,500 feet (460 meters) below the Earth's surface. **Shafts** are built to carry miners and equipment to dig out the coal.

Coal is then taken to power plants by train, barge, or truck. At the power plant, coal is burned in a boiler to make steam. Steam is sent through a turbine to generate electricity. Electricity is carried through power lines. Electricity gives power to many things, including street lamps, refrigerators, and computers.

About 40 percent of electricity used in the United States comes from coal. The U.S. government estimates that there is enough coal left for another 250 years of use. But as natural gas is used up, the rate of coal use will likely increase. The fossil fuels that provide electricity will one day run out.

**mine**—a place where workers dig up materials that are underground

**shaft**—an opening or passageway to a mine

This machine crushes and grinds coal into smaller pieces.

# CHAPTER 3

# The Effects of Fossil Fuels

.............................. Mining for fossil fuels poses dangers to humans and the environment.

Finding fossil fuels and digging them out of the Earth are risky and difficult tasks. These processes pose threats to miners and the environment. When burned to create energy, fossil fuels release gases that impact all living beings on Earth.

## Drilling and Mining

Coal is mined in many parts of the world. China and the United States are the largest producers of coal. Coal miners often work long hours without fresh air. They breathe in dust and tiny bits of coal. Over time, coal miners may suffer from "black lungs." This disease causes the lungs to stop working. There is no cure. Mine explosions and collapses are daily threats to miners.

# Deadly Sound

*Sound waves help engineers find oil and gas buried in the sea. But these waves can shatter the inner ears of whales and other marine mammals. Animals lose their sense of direction and head toward land. Animals stranded on land can die of starvation and heat exposure.*

Drilling for oil is also dangerous and potentially harmful to the environment. Pipes can burst, contaminating nearby land and water. Elements that are toxic to plants, animals, and humans are released.

Natural gas is usually found near oil. Pipelines that carry natural gas can leak, catch fire, or explode. Some ways of extracting natural gas, including fracking, can harm the environment. Fracking is a process in which rocks deep below the surface of Earth are broken apart. This allows more access to natural gas. Scientists have concluded that fracking can contaminate water supplies and cause earthquakes.

Fracking has allowed more access to oil and natural gas below the surface of Earth.

## Spills and Accidents

Many times fossil fuels are mined in areas far from where they will be used. Fossil fuels must be transported and processed before they can be used. During these procedures, accidents and spills happen often. These cause major damage to the environment and put humans and wildlife in danger.

Coal must be washed before it can be burned for use. The dirty water, called coal slurry, sometimes spills into rivers and streams. The water becomes polluted and is a threat to the life within and around it for several decades.

Coal slurry is dumped into this lake in North Carolina.

16

:.. The oil rig Deepwater Horizon burns over the Gulf of Mexico after it exploded in 2010.

Accidents and spills also happen during oil drilling and transporting. In April 2010 an accident on the Gulf coast of the United States leaked 210 million gallons (800 million liters) of oil into the sea. Oil is still present on about 200 miles (320 kilometers) of the coast. Millions of fish, birds, and mammals died. The harmful effects of the oil spill will remain for several generations.

## Changing Air

Fossil fuels must be burned to create energy. But the burning comes at a cost to the environment. Every time fossil fuels are used, harmful substances are released into the air.

Power plants release steam that pollutes and warms the air.

When coal, oil, and natural gas are burned, many harmful gases are released into the air. One of those gases is carbon dioxide. Greater use of fossil fuels has increased the levels of carbon dioxide in the air. Carbon dioxide is a gas that humans exhale. Some carbon dioxide in the air is natural. But today there is about 50 percent more carbon dioxide than there was 40 years ago. Too much carbon dioxide in the environment affects Earth in many ways. Temperatures are rising. Air is polluted. Ocean water is changing. Life is at risk.

Experts believe exhaust from cars is causing more people to suffer from diseases such as asthma.

## A Warmer Planet

The most drastic effect of more carbon dioxide in the air is **global warming**. Global warming is the slow rise in Earth's average temperature that has taken place over the last century. Global warming happens when **greenhouse gases** trap extra heat from the sun inside the Earth's atmosphere. Greenhouse gases, which include carbon dioxide, are found naturally on Earth. These gases help keep Earth warm enough for plants to grow and people and animals to live. This is called the **greenhouse effect**. But too many greenhouse gases, caused by burning fossil fuels and other human activities, have caused worldwide **climate change**. The slight increase in Earth's temperature has impacted the climate in many ways. Today Earth sees more droughts, more severe storms, and more flooding.

**global warming**—a rise in the average worldwide temperature

**greenhouse gas**—gas in a planet's atmosphere that traps heat energy from the sun

**greenhouse effect**—a warming effect that happens when certain gases in Earth's atmosphere absorb heat and make the air warmer

**climate change**—a significant change in Earth's climate over a period of time

.... An increase in Earth's temperatures has led to more flooding.

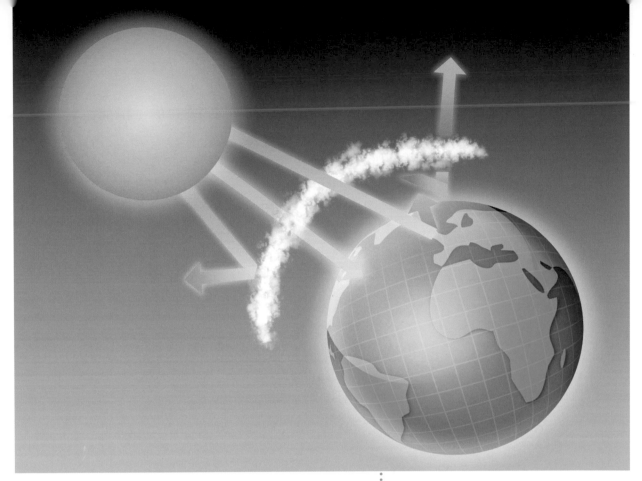

Ozone occurs naturally and helps protect Earth. Too much ozone, though, is harmful.

## Ozone

Ozone forms a protective layer above Earth. It absorbs most of the sun's harmful rays before they reach Earth. But too much ozone too close to the Earth harms people, animals, and crops. Cars and other vehicles release gases that react with heat and sunlight. This creates extra ozone. Extra ozone can irritate a person's lungs, causing coughing, a sore throat, and a heavy feeling in the chest. Symptoms are worse in people who are already sick and can cause permanent lung damage.

ozone—a form of oxygen that exists in Earth's atmosphere in small amounts and contributes in a small way to the greenhouse effect

## Smog

The word *smog* was first used to describe the mixing of smoke from burning coal and fog. Smog today forms when the gases released from burning fossil fuels react with sunlight. Smog is most common in cities with a lot of industry and traffic. These include the U.S. city of Los Angeles and worldwide cities such as London, England; Beijing, China; and Mexico City, Mexico. Smog is unsightly and also dangerous. It damages lungs and causes eye and nose irritation.

## FACT

*The Great Smog of 1952 was caused when the smoke from burning coal covered all of London, England. More than 4,000 people died of respiratory-related diseases after breathing in the toxic smog.*

Many of the world's large cities are dealing with smog, including Beijing.

...... The effects of acid rain can be seen on these statues.

## Ocean Acidification

The oceans absorb a lot of the extra carbon dioxide that's released into the air. The carbon-rich water reacts with salt and sunlight to form carbonic acid. Studies show that carbonic acid harms the shells of oysters and snails. Many fish die in the changing water conditions.

## Acid Rain

Burning fossil fuels also generates acids that contribute to acid rain. Gases react with water droplets before falling to Earth as acid rain. Buildings and sculptures made from limestone begin to dissolve in the acid rain.

# CHAPTER 4

# Saving Energy, Saving Earth

People are using fossil fuels fast. Once fossil fuels are gone, they are gone forever. Most energy used on Earth comes from fossil fuels. Few options for **renewable energy** are currently available. Scientists are working hard to develop clean and **sustainable** energy sources. The U.S. Department of Energy is working on ways to make sustainable energy more available. Where will energy come from in the future?

**renewable energy**—power from sources that will not be used up, such as wind, water, and the sun

**sustainable**—able to keep for a long time

.....These windmills in Spain generate clean and sustainable electricity.

## Clean and Renewable Energy

Clean energy does not produce any carbon dioxide. Therefore, it does not cause temperatures on Earth to rise. The sun, wind, and sea all can provide energy that is clean and renewable.

Solar panels and solar power stations collect heat and energy from the sun's light. The heat and light energy can be used to heat water and make electricity. Wind turbines use wind to generate electricity. However, they only work well in windy places. Tidal turbines are similar to wind turbines. They work under the sea to catch energy from the ocean's tides. Since ocean tides never stop moving, this energy source is constantly available. A geothermal power station uses the heat of molten rocks underground to generate electricity. These work best in places where the molten rock lies close to the Earth's surface. Clean energy isn't commonly used now, but scientists are working on ways to make it cost less and more widely available.

Solar panels collect ····· energy from the sun that can be used for heat and electricity.

## Using Less, Cleaning Up

Burning fossil fuels has permanently changed the land, air, and water. But it's not too late. Scientists are working to develop alternate fuel sources. People are using less fossil fuels and cleaning up the Earth. Every country must work together to clean the land, air, and water and to stop more damage. What changes must be made?

## Drive Less, Drive Differently

Vehicles are one of the biggest contributors to the harm that comes from burning fossil fuels. However, there are ways to cut back or stop the amount of harm they cause.

**Hybrid** cars are one option. Hybrid cars use less fuel and emit less carbon dioxide. These cars use gasoline and electricity at the same time. Other cars do not run on gas but on batteries charged by electricity.

Scientists are working on developing cars that run on other energy sources. These include solar energy, **ethanol**, and oil extracted from algae. These fuels burn more cleanly and require less use of fossil fuels.

...... An electric car is charged at an electric power station.

**hybrid**—a mix of two different types; hybrid engines run on electricity and gasoline

**ethanol**—a fuel made from crops such as corn and sugarcane

# A Better Brazil

*In Brazil about 90 percent of cars sold in the country can run on either oil or ethanol. These cars are known as "flex fuel" cars. Brazil also requires older cars to have converters that will reduce the harmful gas emitted from the cars' tail pipes.*

## Better Buildings

There are several ways to update buildings to make them more energy efficient. Many new buildings are also designed to be more efficient. The more efficient buildings are, the less energy they will use. Better insulation is one way to make a building more efficient. Good insulation keeps cold air out in the winter, and warm air out in the summer.

## Work for Cleaner Energy

Clean-burning electricity sources are currently not available in many areas. In the meantime, there are things people can do to help slow down the use of fossil fuels. There are many ways people can conserve energy by using less. People can also promote the use of better energy by pushing the government to fund and create laws around clean energy.

Many homes and businesses are now built to be more efficient and use better energy sources.

## Simple Changes, Big Differences

Changes must occur around the world before everyone can start using cleaner fuels. But just one person can still make a difference. There are small things everyday people can do to use less energy and help keep Earth clean.

Turn off computer and video games when finished. Turn off the lights when leaving a room. This helps to conserve energy.

Don't leave the refrigerator door open. The fridge needs more energy to cool again.

Unplug appliances that aren't in use. Even if they are turned off, some appliances still use up energy when plugged into an outlet.

During summer open windows in the evening and early morning. Shut the windows and close the blinds during hot parts of the day. This uses less air conditioning.

Walk or ride bikes when traveling shorter distances.

Use cold or warm water in laundry machines. Hang clothes to dry outside on warm days. Hot water and clothes dryers use a lot of energy.

Take reusable bags when shopping. Oil is used to make plastic grocery bags.

In many parts of the world, people are dependent on fossil fuels. Fossil fuels are needed for transportation and to light and warm homes and other buildings. One day fossil fuels will be gone. In the meantime, using them will continue to harm the land, air, and water. People around the world are making changes to bring better energy and a cleaner planet to the future.

# Glossary

**climate change** (KLY-muht CHAYNJ)—a significant change in Earth's climate over a period of time

**diesel** (DEE-zuhl)—a heavy fuel that burns to make power; many semitrucks run on diesel fuel

**energy** (E-nuhr-jee)—the ability to do work, such as moving things or giving heat or light

**ethanol** (ETH-uh-nal)—a fuel made from crops such as corn and sugarcane

**extract** (EK-strakt)—to remove

**fossil fuel** (FAH-suhl FYOOLZ)—natural fuel formed from the remains of plants and animals; coal, oil, and natural gas are fossil fuels

**global warming** (GLOH-buhl WAR-meeng)—a rise in the average worldwide temperature

**greenhouse effect** (GREEN-houss uh-FEKT)—a warming effect that happens when certain gases in Earth's atmosphere absorb heat and make the air warmer

**greenhouse gas** (GREEN-houss GASS)—gas in a planet's atmosphere that traps heat energy from the sun

**hybrid** (HY-brid)—a mix of two different types; hybrid engines run on electricity and gasoline

**methane** (meth-AYN)—colorless, flammable gas produced by decay of plant and animal matter

**mine** (MINE)—a place where workers dig up materials that are underground

**ozone** (OH-zohn)—a form of oxygen that exists in Earth's atmosphere in small amounts and contributes in a small way to the greenhouse effect

**photosynthesis** (foh-toh-SIN-thuh-siss)—the process by which plants make food using sunlight, carbon dioxide, and water

**purify** (PYOOR-uh-fye)—to make something clean

**refinery** (ree-FINE-uhr-ee)—a place where oil is made into gasoline and other products

**renewable energy** (ri-NOO-uh-buhl EN-er-jee)—power from sources that will not be used up, such as wind, water, and the sun

**shaft** (SHAFT)—an opening or passageway to a mine

**sustainable** (suh-STAY-nuh-bel)—able to keep for a long time

# Critical Thinking Using the Common Core

1. Discuss two of the major problems with humans' reliance on fossil fuels for energy that are covered in the text. Identify and explain both of these problems. (Key Idea and Details)

2. Reread the text on page 26 about better vehicles and study the photo. What are the potential benefits of driving cars that don't require gasoline and what, if any, might be the downsides? Support your answer with information from the text and other print and reliable Internet sources. (Integration of Knowledge and Ideas)

3. Now that you've read the text, give three suggestions on how to cope with the need for renewable energy in the wake of diminishing fossil fuels. Support your answer. (Integration of Knowledge and Ideas)

# Read More

**Bang, Molly, and Penny Chisolm.** *Buried Sunlight: How Fossil Fuels Have Changed the Earth.* New York: The Blue Sky Press, 2014.

**Gorman, Jacqueline Laks.** *Fossil Fuels.* What If We Do Nothing? Pleasantville, N.Y.: Gareth Stevens Publishing, 2009.

**Ollhoff, Jim.** *Fossil Fuels.* Future Energy. Edina, Minn.: ABDO Publishing, 2010.

# Internet Sites

FactHound offers a safe, fun way to find Internet sites related to this book. All of the sites on FactHound have been researched by our staff.

Here's all you do:

Visit www.facthound.com

Type in this code: 9781491420379

# Index